THE ANNIE POEMS

THE
ANNIE
POEMS

ANNE CAMERON

Harbour Publishing Co Ltd
1987

The Annie Poems
Copyright © Canada 1987 Anne Cameron
All rights reserved

Published by Harbour Publishing Co Ltd
Box 219, Madeira Park, BC V0N 2H0

Cover painting by Gaye Hammond
Printed and bound in Canada

Canadian Cataloguing in Publication Data

Cameron, Anne, 1938—
    The Annie poems
    ISBN 0-920080-91-X
I. Title.
PS8555.A44A73 1986   C811'.54   C86-091504-2
PR9199.3.C3A73 1986

CONTENTS

The Sickness That Has No Name

Mother of All

Annie Poems

The Sickness That Has No Name

Riding To Town With My Mother

Riding to town with my mother

watching familiar streets
flanked by familiar yards
recognizing people on the sidewalks
a lifetime of acquaintances
Women I knew as girls
when we were all in school together
look, now, so
. . . like my mother. . .
caught between wanting to be people
and wanting to be
lost in the crowd
The women I know best
do not look like this
they have lines and wrinkles
from laughing and squinting in the sun
their mouths are unpainted
and do not droop down
as if gravity
controlled all situations
and was
obligatory
The women I know best
speak from their chests
not from their adenoids
and they laugh
from the gut
or
even lower
The women I know best
walk freely, loosely
claiming their space
taking their place
they do not
apologize
for existing

My mother is saying something to me
I turn
am struck with pain and loss
with confusion and panic
Who is this
stranger
driving this car?
I recognize nothing
and for a terrible moment
I am alone in a car
with a woman I do not know

it passes
almost

Yuquatl

Only the dead
have not deserted you
Only the dead
become artifacts
and archeological finds
The dead
    and my spirit
living here now
I sank
to the sea kingdom
and the blackfish king
wished to wed
But the cormorants
showed the way
their eyes no longer blinded
and I followed
though my own eyes
no longer see clearly
They watch me, these people
watch me with sideways eyes
and dread
those of my dreams
as are true
Only the dead
have not deserted you
The dead
and my spirit
which longs
for the undersea kingdom
I left

I Didn't Want To Go

I didn't want to go
The blind cormorant people
could not and would not
be resisted

The sun here is cold
and the water dries your blood
You are always
frightened

The cormorant people show the way
and if you are not a coward
you can follow them

Past the pitfalls and crevices
past the lair of the blackfish king
to the storage place
of the snowy otter fur

And when you have it you know
you can never keep it
It is too much

You will never drown in water
and at night
the voices will tell you
the names you must know

People will fear you
will look at you
with cormorant eyes
and stand sideways when you pass

Your dreams will be true
and that, too, is fearful
But you cannot refuse to go
for the cormorant people
will not be denied

and you will not drown... in water

Sickness

Wind from the inlet, thick with salt smell
trees soughing and protesting; in the few
pauses between gusts the rattles and clumps
from the mill; nothing on the radio but static
and outside the purple night swallows the town

Purple night swallowing and the wind devouring
last week half the porch roof
went
only a few shards left, the other half still there
absurd and ineffectual, challenging tonight's storm

Let me curl close to your back
press your buttocks against my belly
I need the comfort of flesh and warmth
The purple is eating the world

   Sleep is elusive now
   breathing loud in my ears
   the rush of blood in my veins
   my teeth hard and sharp
   my nails scratching my skin
     let me cuddle your back
     I need the warmth of touch

We are survivors of an ice age
kept alive only by our secret fire
the wind shrieks
through the cathedral columns
of our bones
the curved arch
of our ribs

Purple devouring the world
and all our being blowing in the gale
I tell you—how often—this wind affects me
and you talk of atmospheric pressure and
bionic regulation and
do not understand
when I say It Is Blowing The Wrong Way

ii

Was the earth born in storms?
The gulls flee inland
Do the whales frolic in the combers?

I am a rock
Cold. Immovable
Moss grows upon me
Rain falls on me
Wind. . . blows over

    Do not lean on me
    There are red droplets on my chin
    and raw meat in my belly

Turn to me
  Let me turn you to me

I have need of your warmth
  The wind is killing me
  The old cold is killing me

    You have no warmth to give me

iii

I am huddled in the cave
waiting for the ice to thaw
The fur pelt on your chest is
flattening my breasts, if you would
admit you know me, the ice would thaw
But it is cold and I am alone, my
thighs gripping ice haunches, my calves
crossed over yours, my fingers feeling
    cold

When the cold enters me I leave the cave
and learn for myself the weaving of weirs
the lonely cry of the eagle, the mocking laughter
of cormorant and the peace that brings quiet
  I plant the roots deep in the earth
  set the hills in their places
  and in my eye the falcon climbs

I am the spirit face you carve
to protect yourself
I am the phratry you paint on your skin
to comfort yourself
I am the amulet you wear around your neck

I am the song the whale sings
as she gives birth
I am the blood that stains the waters
and the afterbirth she severs

I am the hand holding the knife
you hold to my throat
I am the scar you call my smile

iv
Press your flesh against me
The cold is trapped in my throat
I breathe ice and sweat snow

And outside the wind blows the Wrong Way

Cure

To be cured of the sickness that has no name
requires meditation, special diet
bloodletting, and incantation
      — magic four —

The Old Woman is waiting when we arrive
walking backward through the door
seeing the world we are leaving as we approach
the world we will enter
impressing that which we leave on our minds
lest we not be able to return, having
forgotten from whence we came

The Old Woman looks calm and her title
does not signify her age. She moves between
her fortieth and fiftieth year, her eyes
piercing argyllite darts, cutting through
my face and into my head. Part of
my mind says I Know Her, have seen her
in the town, taking her grandchildren to the circus
waiting in line with them to see Snow White
Part of my mind says She Is A Stranger
a part phantom being from years long lost

The Old Woman is expressionless
She watches as the disciples
remove my clothes. I am aware of the
paleness of my skin, their hands dark on my arm

The Old Woman sits
The disciples, wordless, bid me sit
their hands putting gentle pressure
on my shoulders, removing the
band from my head, my hair
falling free, hanging loose

Old Woman takes herbs from her pouch
drops them in the fire between us
The disciples begin to chant
softly, the suggestion of rhythm

distracting me, a strange chord structure
not octave chords but fifths. Or fourths
The herb smoke glitters in the air
suggestions of prisms, rainbows, sunlight
caught in the mist of the waterfall

My skin is warm. My eyes heavy
The disciples' chant has entered my head
a soft pulsing in my temples joining
with the sound from the small drum
the young woman is stroking with
the tips of her fingers

The Old Woman sits, blinking slowly
in the folds of her simple brown robe
her hands lie calm, palms up, and
the strands of my life are caught there

A disciple makes marks upon my skin
hemlock branches leaving fine red welts
and a part of me says This Ought To Hurt—
but it doesn't

The Old Woman begins to speak
using words from a language I do not know
glottal stops and the "s" and "sh" sounds
altered, become neither "s" nor "sh" but . . .
something else . . . and the "g" or "j" joined
with a sort of a—click—the speech
pattern strange in my anglo ears
familiar and fitting within my breast
and my eyes fill with tears
            she has welcomed me

The Old Woman fixes her eyes on mine
Words and meanings become unimportant
we communicate in a better way
mind touching mind, soul touching soul
images and shadows in my head
a burning behind my eyes
my arms, legs, my body become heavy
head drooping, and always the images

always the images

When did you become afflicted with
the sickness that has no name

Grandmother, I am frightened
I have been to the kingdom beneath the sea
and my dreams are true. They look at me
with sideways eyes and ask of me
that which I cannot give
At night I waken wet with sweat, the
breath of Tsonoqua warm on my back
and I think I see the Stlalacum lurking
in the folds of the curtains
Grandmother, I am frightened
I move among them but am not of them
and always their eyes demand and expect
they Expect, they Expect and I am
afraid I have leeches stuck on my skin
When I speak to them they understand my words
but do not understand what I say

When did you become afflicted with
the sickness that has no name

My arms are jerked by hot white wires
my legs moved by burning tongs
my back is flayed and someone is
dancing, someone is dancing, someone is
        being thrown high in the air
        caught by strong women's hands
thrown back into the air
to fall and be caught again

and birds with the bodies of women
are flying through the air, and the
hemlock switches are marking my skin

and someone is dancing

Grandmother I am afraid

When did you become afflicted with
the sickness that has no name

and the figure dancing
    the figure flailed
    the figure weeping
has found the words of her song

Grandmother, I was born afflicted
I   was   born
    afflicted

The song stops, the dancers freeze
the drum is silent, the fire doused

Old Woman rises, nods, smiles, and
rubs a salve on my back. The
bleeding stops, the stinging stops and
she says
    We are never cured
    we only learn to Endure

And she is gone

We walk through the door backward
leaving the worm dying in the ashes

Old Woman

Old Woman
is working
gathering
the frayed ends of dreams
the ravelled edges of hopes
re-weaving
your soul
Her face
this pale moonlit night
is sharp and spare
her eyes
deep shadowed hollows
her mouth
pursed and wrinkled
and as she weaves
she hums a salt sea melody
that tells of cedar and rock
and the twisted
granite-wood arbutus
clinging tenaciously to cliff face
perched above the crashing waves
gnarled and bent by hail
She does not
waste her time
in recriminations
She does not
waste your time
with sympathy
She hums her song
her gnarled-root fingers
weaving your mind
making whole again
your fabric of being

Old Woman Sat in Her Dugout

Old Woman sat in her dugout
her cowl over her head
the calm sea flat as glass
beneath the stalegray sky
In her nose the scent of evergreen
from the wooded shore
the scent of moss and fern
the sharp salty tang
of surf and kelp
and the first hint
of changing wind

Her eyes, glittering from
within her hood, saw the
cormorant and gull head inland
the seal and otter head for
their rookeries
and beneath the slick surface
of the sea the water began
to heave uneasily
like the belly of a woman
in the first stages of childbirth

She stirred in her dugout
a slight smile of anticipation
shifting the folds and wrinkles
of her time-crinkled face

She shook her cowl
back slightly from her face
her spare features feeling the
first sharp gusts of wind
the folds of her robe stirring
with expectations

The sea quickened, the slick
swells began heaving with rhythmic power
surging with endless passion
carving deeper the lines already
etched in basalt and slate

The wind pushed spray and rain
lifted the mist from the sea
and swirled it with rash abandon
over the slowly straightening form
She grinned, stood erect, her robe wet
its folds dripping, the salt
fluid streaming from cowl to sleeve, from sleeve to hem
until the very dugout was drenched
and heaving in the tossing waves

She began to sway to the rhythm
of her personal song, to move her
body to the beat of the storm
and the insistent coursing of her
own blood in her veins. Her mouth
opened and her spirit chant
issued from her lips, merging with
the sound of the wind, the feel of rain
and salt spray

The sea churned, the wavetips
became white froth,the dugout heaved
and as the storm reached its peak
Old Woman's chant became a cry of
victory and celebration.
She had—again—Endured
she had—again—challenged
and triumphed.

Old Woman Looked At Me

The Old Woman looked at me
puzzled
and asked
Why do you ignore
your grandmothers?
They miss you
and their grandmothers ask them
why you do not love
your own
spirits

And so I told her
I do not know them
Their language
is denied me
Their customs
have been buried
They live
in another place
and I
was born here
am connected here

The Old Woman smiled
and said
but you know language
does not matter
in that other place
and what has been buried
will always
resurface

I could only trust her
as I had always trusted her
and
when you trust
you trust all the way

and I am waiting

Punishment

They found a stranger
lurking near the village
his skin darkstained
with the blood
of the slain child
  . . . he wanted me to
      he cried repeatedly
      he wanted me to
      but then he got scared
      and I had to stop
      his screaming. . .

They took him
to the sea
stood him
in water to his hips
at low tide
A thong from his hair
to his bound wrists
face turned upward
to the rain
feet fastened
to large rocks
his hamstrings
severed
his testicles
hanging from his neck
  . . . he wanted me to
      but then he got scared
      and I had to stop
      his screaming. . .

They went back to the village
leaving him
to the rising tide
his dead seeds
cooling
against his chest

I went to him
my clamshell knife
in my hand
my words killed him
my clamshell knife
merely released his
spirit through the
skin of his throat

my words killed him
. . . I wish I'd never known you. . .
my words killed
my brother
. . . he wanted me to
and I had to stop
his screaming. . .

Tem Eyos Ki

Tem Eyos Ki learned love
in the waiting house
surrounded by women
and when she came back
she was a woman struck by lightning
She led the women away from the village
away from pots and pans and duties and obedience
into a forest where they frolicked with the children
and learned how love could really be
When the men sought them out
a magic dugout came from the sky
and Tem Eyos Ki leaped into it
singing
and rode off above the rain forest

She visited with the magic people
learned songs from them

At night I could hear her
and I yearned

I Waken With the Smell of Gravedirt

I waken with the smell of gravedirt
and the dust of death on my skin
The bones of forgotten corpses
dance in caves beneath the sea
and HuHu picks her teeth and laughs
while the shaman bleeds
trying to stop the wheel from turning

There are no totems for the fireweed clan
we burned them when the healers perished
At night my skin is greasy with fear
and the smell of me is unpleasant
Sometimes I wonder if I will ever find
my way back from that place
or if I will stay and only my bones
and meat, hair, nails, and skin
be left in this bed

On the nights you sleep with me
there is birdsong and blossomscent
and I lie in warm darkness

HuHu

That one
is often insane with rage
flies at us
trying to sink her beak
through our skullshells
to peck into and eat
our brains
Those ones
who see only with their eyes
might think that one is Raven
Those ones
who hear only with their ears
might never recognize the call of HuHu
Your blue eyes see clearly
and your shell ears hear past the wind
Sometimes
you take my fear from me
and bury it laughing
When my head aches
I tell that one to leave me in peace
and I lie alone in my bed
wondering why my own eyes
are so often drawn to shadows

I Am the One They Warn Of

I am the one they warn of
I am the one whose name they use
to frighten disobedient children
Be careful they say
or she'll get you!
Don't stay out after sunset
or she'll catch you!
Go to bed on time
or she'll find you!
Eat your meals, wash behind your ears
tell the truth, do as you're told
or she'll grab you

I am the one
whose voice you hear
in the untamed night wind
I am the one
lurking
just beyond the edge
of the clearing
staring
from the rain forest
face hidden
in moss and fog

I am the one
comes to you at night
and creeps into your dreams
I invade your most private moments
and tempt you
with visions
of naked breasts
round belly
wide hips
muscular thighs

I am the mouth on your nipple
I am the tongue teasing your navel
I am the one stroking you

stroking you stroking you stroking
and it is my soft laughter you hear
when you waken
burning

I am the one they warned you about
the one
you cannot admit
you want

Petroglyph Eyes

I
am the woman
they call The Threat
the witch hag
they wish to kill

I
am the voice in the wind
the hands reaching
like claws
in the vines across the path

I am the one they fear
the one they wish to kill
to rip open
with their clamshell knives

I live away from their villages
digging roots with my bare hands
setting snares
breaking small furry necks
and drinking rich warm blood

My father murdered my mother
then lived with her ghost
He seduced the wives
of other men
and terrified the world
with his rage

My father assassinated laughter
and turned song and music
into screams and sobs

He was insane
and his madness
contagious

My mother
lived as a ghost
for two lifetimes

Hers and mine
Her eyes
accuse the world

I do not know her

I know only her ghost
It stirs in her grave
and begs for release

I could free her
or kill her
but I refuse

she Expects too much

ii
If I could believe my birth
I could accept my life

My brothers
died fighting
for no cause at all

their blood spilled to the earth
their eyes stare sightless
their voices
beg me to join them

they say
we hunger
for the warm maiden's touch
they say
we yearn
for
    everything

their blood
drips from my eyes

her blood
runs in my veins

his blood
I drank

iii
The Others
built villages
gathered clams
hunted mowitch and whale
and danced

built fires
and danced
chasing away the cold
singing
and dancing

singing
and dancing
until
his madness
stilled their songs

we
killed their children
killed them
until
all my brothers
were gone

iv
My mother
crawled into her cave-grave
and waits for me

My father
brought me his idea
brought me
his desire

and I drank his blood

his desire sickened me

I
am the woman
they call
The Threat
the woman
they wish to kill

When they hear my voice
they reach for their axes
they reach for their spears
they hide their daughters

Their sons
flex their muscles
and talk bravely
in loud voices
bragging
and spitting
and waiting
to violate my body

Their wives
remember my words
remember
the country from which I come
and curse my name

Their daughters
either fear me
or envy
what they see as
my freedom

I
warm the bed of no man
I prepare meals
only for myself
I
do not swell
with their sons

nor receive
the lunge of their lust

I walk the beach barefoot
even after dark
and
sometimes
when the moonlight gleams
on the bare skin
of an adventuresome
runaway daughter
some
free spirit
who
yearns to feel sand
between her bare toes
and who insists
the night, too, is ours
or
who resents
the plans her father makes
sometimes
when she bathes
in the combers

I come from the forest

I sing to her of freedom
and choice
I sing to her
of my dead brothers
and the taste of my
father's blood

and our laughter
almost
erases the sound
of his mad rage

v
In the morning they find her gone
and search

following her footsteps
seeing the marks on the beach
where she
danced
with me
and we celebrated
and they know
she will not return
to their cold beds

They rage
and call me The Threat
and plan to kill me

I am not afraid

I would welcome their death
Until then
I celebrate life

I Watch the Ghosts of My Brothers

On this beach I watch the ghosts of my brothers
still casting nets in wraith-fog
pursuing phantom silver
My brothers who died
for no good reason at all
You must understand
the lawgiver King was insane
death dripped from his lips
horror slipped from his tongue
and his rules were assassins
They, like innocent fools
obeyed their king

The flags flew and the people danced
wine was spilled freely and the streets
were halcyon swirls for days

I have no brothers now and want none
My sisters bleed to death regularly
their faces pale and resigned, their eyes empty
They do not even know they have lost
something
But their children are well-behaved and tidy
and their nice husbands always have
fresh baked bread

I am the only one who is insane
The one who sees with tangent focused eyes
and it is not their fault
if I walk in the rain
or sit in a cave
eating raw meat
and singing
discordant songs

ii
My mother watched her sons
watched them follow her brothers
listened to the mad lawgiver
then stuffed her ears with pollen

31

turned her eyes inward
and waits now to turn to dust
Her blood runs thinner each day
and sometimes it is easier to see
her shadow than it is to see her
She hears voices and reasons
I cannot hear, she follows paths
I cannot see and our language
is a mystery each to the other

    You
    ride across my mind
    the perfume of flowers
    you have nightstars
    caught in your hair
    you make me a gift
    of cloud and mist
    your fingerprints etched
    on the pores of my inner skin
    you are sea foam
    you are moonlight
    you are
    that wonder just beyond
    the reach of my hand
    a quicksilver sliding
    from my grasp
    more real
    than law or reason

iii
At night I leave my cave
and limp through the night
moving toward the mountain
moving in search of you

    Here is the lake
    silver in the starlight
    trees loom like predators
    the darkness pulsing, waiting
    In those shadows
    blacker than night

hidden in cobwebs
captive of spiders
the dead children
turn vacant white faces
to an uncaring moon
their open mouths
black holes
scream silently
and the maiden
bleeds unmourned
her death
welcome release
finally

You ride in this forest
I hear your footsteps faint
the echo of your laughter
part of what I see, what I cannot see
part of that beyond my sight
hidden in my head
and I lurch after the fading music
that is the uncaring laughter from your lips

iv
Through the night
toward the mountain
stumbling after the sound
you leave behind you
following the scent
of unblossomed flowers
but
you are too swift
I limp too slowly
and so I return to the beach
and my hollow-eyed vigil
sitting in the sand
watching ghosts with fognets
casting eternally casting

Sometimes
in that time before I
crawl back into my cave

to hide from the daylight
and the acid eyes of
those I cannot understand
Sometimes
on that wet cold beach
shivering and lonely
you
sneak up behind me, silent
and then your arms
embrace me, your lips
sear the side of my neck
your kiss burns like lightning
and
    you laugh and vanish again

v

Around the mouth of my cave
I hang bright scraps of cloth
shards of broken mirror, bits of ribbon
a few small bells and feathers
taken from the breasts of brilliant birds
I decorate the entrance
trying to entice you
trying to invite you
but you ignore me

    Once you came close
    and left flowers
    on a stump
    and bloody bits of
    fur on a string
    I wear them around my neck
    and dream of you

Inside my cave
I have treasures
And there is a song
I would sing for you
It is not a song of my brothers
It is not a song of the mad king

It is not a song of my sisters
Nor a song of my mother
Nor any of them
The song I would sing you
Is a song of warmth
of laughter and trust, of
mouth and tongue, breath and sweat
a song
I will sing for you
One day

Mad Woman

In the village
they frighten their children
into obedience
by warning them
of the mad woman
who lurks
in the forest shadows
with fangs bared
and stomach
hungry

I am that woman

There is dried blood
in my hair
and shards of
undigested gristle
in my gut

I saw my mother
lying where she fell
in the moss
A small green frog
nestled comfortably
in her gaping eye socket
Small furry animals
had disturbed her bones
Her lower jaw
was missing, and
when I spoke to her
she could not answer

I searched
three days and two nights
but could not find it

I found
the long bone
of her upper leg
her knuckles
and six
of her vertebrae

Come with me I said
but she just lay there
Lazy
The small green frog
winked at me
I did not wink back
I had not come
in search of frogs

My father
has been gone
almost long enough
for the memory of his madness
to fade

and the scars
to stop throbbing

Some nights
the scars on my wrists
itch
and I scratch
until they bleed
again

I have other wounds
They itch
I cannot reach them
to scratch

They bleed
dust

Will the frog
nestle comfortably
in my eyesocket?

Will he feel cold?

Will the children
of the village
frighten him

or he
they?

Hecate

cement forms
derelict in the water
huge metal vats
unused and rusting
houses
empty houses
floors tilted
stairways
staggering
windows
like eyeless holes
in a bleached
   skull
I walked in the lupine field
picked blackberries
wondered if the bear who left
his droppings
would return
and reclaim his bush
feeling
eyes
from the forest
eyes
from inside the
empty houses
eyes
slanted
and dead
staring
and I panicked

I Am Here Among You

I am here
among you
I have been obedient
gone into your churches
my skinny little-girl legs
covered with dark stockings
my tight little-girl body
covered with long sleeved blouse
dark pleated over-tunic
my scrawny child throat
sticking up above a proper uniform
and I learned the verses
I joined the choir
and made
a joyful noise unto your lord

I am here
among you
I have learned to smile
at all the right times
and right people
I always say thank you
I am never boisterous
some even think me
— shy —

I am here
among you
asking that innocent question
that tumbles the house of cards

I am here
among you

I
pagan

Stained Glass and Vaulted Ceiling

The stained glass and vaulted ceiling
of the Anglican church
every High Day and Holy Day
was
magic
bright red, rich blue, vibrant purple
gold and silver, ermine and silk
altar cloths and robes
and all the women and children singing
praise while the Archdeacon
walked slowly
to give the sermon
and
bless us

> lord have mercy upon us
> christ have mercy upon us
> lord have mercy upon us

> > i believe in god the father almighty
> > maker of heaven and earth
> > and in jesus christ his only son our lord

> have mercy upon us

how we sang and how we believed
and then
belief was gone

I, who knew all the verses
I, who knew all the prayers
I, who knew the songs
I, who knew the responses
was told
I
could never wear the robes
or give the sermon
or
be anything
except a nun

Anglican nuns were invisible
they had to be
In all my life
I have yet to know I am seeing one

Is this the reward for belief?
Invisibility?

They told me Eve sinned
and all women
share her sin, her guilt
and cannot be
Archdeacons. Or anything
except
nuns

Poverty, chastity, obedience
was the highest I was allowed
I grew up knowing poverty
If chastity and obedience
were anything similar
I wasn't interested

When faith is gone you are left with
fear
what if. . . .
what if. . . .
what if. . . .

they really are right?

what if. . . hell. . .

         christ have mercy upon us

into this constant confusion
Images of Raven the Trickster
              the Transformer

and the fear
withered

Klopinum told me
we were part of
not apart from
creation

sharing the world
with trees and rocks
with rivers and oceans
with the beach
and
all creatures

were not
in dominion
over
but
interconnected with

and faith
returned

Mother of All

Whenever a Child Is Born

Whenever a child was born
three magic women spirits
gathered by the cradle
showing the child
the three faces of the one mother
The tribal mother
would lift the child
give ceremonious suck
claiming this new person
as a child of the mother
a child of the Great Mother
full citizen of the tribe

Tribal mother
whose husbands had but one function
to provide the seed
and if the tribal mother
did not quicken often enough
or if the children were sickly
or in any way imperfect
the husband
was throttled with a silken cord
and replaced

To each queen
a pleasure-man, trained by the women
to concentrate totally
on the queen's pleasure
to prepare her in every way
for the sperm donor husband
The pleasure man trained by women
to unite energy with the queen
and without sexual union
blaze golden
until the combined soul
rose from their bodies
linked with the all-knowing
and secrets
were revealed

Aya

"A"
Aya, the mother of all things
mother of all wisdom
mother of all courage
        of all strength
            and glory

from you, greek alpha
also called river of birth
            river of creation
    called Styx
river of death
which courses seven times
through the womb of the earth
emerging finally
from death
as life

Aya!
Hail

Abaton

Abaton
earth-womb
we enter to sleep overnight
to incubate
to be visited by
an incubus
who brings us dreams
which dreams
will teach us
how to interpret
dreams
learn the truth
of dreams

incubus
succubis
dream lover
who brings freedom
            passion
            joy

incubus
succubis
earth-womb dream-womb

Abishag

Abishag
chosen for your beauty
to arouse in the aged king
the virility potency fertility
without which
the king is not king
but
sacrifice
Abishag
priestess
surrogate mother
surrogate goddess
without your blessing
without your warmth
the land becomes barren
the people devastated

Two brothers two princes
waited
and when the old king
failed
and died
both princes
lusted
for the kingdom

Solomon was chosen
and crowned by the queen mother
but Adonijah
asked for your hand in marriage
Thus, to protect his throne
Solomon
had Adonijah
murdered
for whoever responded
to your beauty, your heat
was blessed

by the Goddess
beside whom
earthly thrones
are
but
dust

Amazons

Watching television
seeing Khaddafi that mad bastard
drooling terrorism
it is hard to remember
Libya
which used to include all of North Africa
was called the home
of the Amazons
The Greek historians were amazed
by the warlike women of Libya
who today are muffled by veils
subservient and oppressed

It was the Amazons
who made friends with horses
attacked invading footsoldiers
and scattered them

When Hugh Cullan tried to defeat the Celts
it was Nmhain the Amazon and her women
who screamed defiance
and the sound of their voices
killed a hundred warriors

The Christians had to pass laws
forbidding Celtic women
from bearing arms
and after the 9th century
any woman who knew how to defend herself
was labelled "witch"
and burned

If the sound of our rage
can kill one hundred warriors
why
do we not understand more fully
how important it is to them
that we be conditioned
to talk softly, quietly, in high, thin, weak voices

How important to them
that we laugh softly, politely, or not at all

Have you ever listened— truly Listened—
to the voices of black women, of native women
to the voices of dykes

voices from deep in the throat
voices rich as cream
voices pitched low and full

not the least bit
ladylike

but incredibly womanly
Amazonian

Arianrhod

Arianrhod
with your spinning wheel
turning
endlessly
turning
your silver star wheel
turning time and time
turning Time
a silver ship carrying the dead
taking them
to the moon
the moon which lies
behind the milky way
milky way
cosmic wheel of the zodiac
spinning the fate
the destiny of our lives
the manner and time of our death
waiting
to sail us
to that cool silver land
called
Hymenia

Artemis

Artemis
moon goddess
who gave birth to all creatures
a torso covered with breasts
who nurtures all things
Artemis
also called
Dianna
huntress of all things
killer of all creatures
known also
as Cutter or Butcher

Leader of the midnight hunt
accompanied by fierce black dogs
Great SheBear, Ursa Major
Queen of Heaven
Holy Mother Ma Tsu P'o
protects seafarers, rules the weather
Mother of mercy
and of death

Patroness of fertility and birth
of nurturing and harvesting
Artemis
who brings together
milk and blood
Hail!

Ceridwen

Ceridwen
triple goddess, sacred sow
terrifying white
corpse eating
cauldron carrying
from you we come
to you we return
Ceridwen
mother of many
who eats her own young
your cauldron contains
inspiration
protectress of bards
of poets and talespinners
Ceridwen
you turn the circle of creation
from birth through life to death

Chang-O

Chang-O
pale white goddess of moonlight
into your care
the sacred ambrosia of immortality

Almond-eyed
jasmine-skinned
more fair than the Lotus

Keeper of life magic
Guardian of eternity
Her consort, the Excellent Archer
grew jealous
coveted
control
coveted control of the ambrosia

quarrelled with her
quarrelled with Chang-O

Pale moon goddess left her consort
lives now on the moon

Some nights
you can see her face
"Look, mommy, look, the woman in the moon"

Some nights
she looks down on us
dispenses
the menstrual blood of immortality
only to women

Only she
Chang-O
has any control
over our bodies

Only she
and ourselves

Keep faith with Chang-O
Give no man control of your body

Chicomecoatl

Chicomecoatl
Heart of the Earth
ancestress of all peoples
Mother of all
seven serpents bring your messages
Chicomecoatl
you spew vengeance from volcanoes
sit in judgement
on all gods
You send your savior-son
as fertility sacrifice
He falls on us
from the sky
Chicomecoatl
mother of rain
mother of all
mother of fire
mother of all

Chomo-Lung-Ma

Chomo-Lung-Ma
Goddess Mother Of The Universe
highest mountain on earth

In 1863
foreign invaders
patriarchs
named you after Sir George Everest

Men of all nations
are obsessed with the thought
of climbing
Chomo-Lung-Ma
Goddess Mother Of The Universe
leaving chocolate bar wrappers
empty oxygen cannisters
and plastic baggies
of their own excrement

Chomo-Lung-Ma
ignores them
sometimes
shrugs
flings these heroes aside

Chomo-Lung-Ma
Goddess Mother Of The Universe

Coatlicue

Coatlicue
born of a volcano, mother of all deities
mother of the moon, the sun, the stars
Her daughter was the Goddess of All Women
and Xochiquetzal intercedes for us
presenting our case to Coatlicue
who receives us back into her body when we have died
who wears a necklace of skulls
who wears a skirt of serpents
who wears a cape of castrated penises
who walks fierce above the clouds
waiting
waiting for the sleeping volcano
to again erupt
waiting for us to awaken
waiting for us to be born of our own volcano
waiting for us to ask Xochiquetzal
to ask her mother
to aid us

Creiddylad

Creiddylad
Queen of the May
first of the three sisters
Every first day of May
the two heroes
fight
First one wins
then the other
over and over
and over and over
and over and
over and over

On the first of May
before the sun has dried the dew
women
hurry outside
to honour
Creiddylad

Wash your face
in May Day dew
and every day of the year
you will become
more blessed

Wash your face
in May Day dew
often enough
you will become

the beautiful Crone

Demeter

De is the delta
the triangle
sign of female genitals
door of birth
door to paradise
Meter is mother
Demeter
womb of the goddess
virgin mother crone
creator preserver destroyer
barley mother
wise one of earth and sea
Melaina the black one
Chthonia the underground one
Erinya the avenger
Carrying dolphin and dove
you gallop in darkness
your mare-headed form
torments sinners in their sleep

Demeter
Corn Mother
Old Woman

we are initiated through secret things
secret things heard
secret things tasted
secret things seen

secret things
experienced

Dzelarhons

Dzelarhons
first wife to be beaten
you took your woven cedar bark hat
said a magic word
and transformed it
into a conical copper hat

Your insane husband
tried to take it
and the hat
flew out of your hand
slammed him alongside his head
dumped him
on his backside

and you left

Dzelarhons
how long did you live in the forest alone?
How long did you endure guilt
and shame? How long did you believe
it was your fault
he had beaten you?

When the mountain spewed fire
you ran to warn the people
and saved their lives

Now
you are Volcano Woman
your breasts
shoot flames
spew
molten rock
you protect women and children
and wreak vengeance on those
who would abuse, rape, or oppress

Dzelarhons
you are not gentle

nor beautiful
nor any of the things
considered
womanly
feminine
correct
acceptable
proper

Dzelarhons
woman
shaman
sister

Dzelarhons
it was the great earthquake
which shattered the rock shelf
and formed the first Island
which catapulted you
from your birthplace
to
that other

and you yearned for home
wept for your aunties
and for the soft mists
of this coast

And so
it was you took a cedar log
burned out the centre
experimenting
failing
trying again
until
finally
you had a dugout

And it was you
brought yourself home again

Seeker
Dreamer

Fisherwomen

It was women harvested the sea
women ruled by the moon
harvesting
tides ruled by the moon
casting nets and plying them
bringing silver bodied fish
glittering like moonbeams
and then
the jealous ones
moved

and fisherwomen
were replaced
by fishermen
even though
the world-wide symbol of the Mother
was the tailless fish
Minaksi is the fish-eyed one,
and Abtu is
the great fish of the Abyss

The Greek word delphos
means womb, means also fish
Themis showed herself as a dolphin
Aphrodite Salacia ruled Fridays
and her people feasted on fish
while celebrating a day of lovemaking
And it is Marina
who brought forth all the fish in the sea
and ordered them to dance
when the moon mother played her song.

The goddess Boann lived as a tree
and her menstrual blood fell in droplets
from the white oak to the river
where migrating salmon swallowed them
protecting the drops of wisdom
until the Celtic women wove and cast nets
to catch the salmon, and, in eating the fish

learned the secrets of moon and star
of blood and milk, of birth and rebirth
and of all things
mysterious

Hag

Death goddess
priestess of sacrifice
on the last night of the old year
hagmenai
we stay together
safe
in merry company
until
after midnight

and haggis
the hag's dish
of chopped organs
reminds us
of the hag

Hag
hawk
to be haggard
is to be
harpy
is to be
wild
is to be
hawklike

mother hawk
kills
rends hot steaming bloody meat
feeds her young

hag
crone
old woman

laugh!

Hel

Warm womb
bubbling cauldron of heat
uterine cave of rebirth
fire mountain
where the souls of the dead women
wait
until such time as the Mother Of All
accedes
and all who were
will be again
There is no fear in that womb
no destruction or danger
for the oven
is the mother
and in former times
the baking of bread
was a religious pursuit
Fornix: oven
Fornicalia: oven feasts
Fornix: furnace
and thus
fornicate

Those who taste the sacred fire of eternity
                    the sacred fire of fornication
will, those priests warn
burn forever in hell

Hel
norse queen of the underworld
where the bubbling cauldron of heat
seethes
in the uterine cave of rebirth
and the souls of the dead Amazons
wait

wait
warm themselves at the sacred fire
of eternity
of fornication

that volcano of woman rage
will erupt
that volcano of woman love
will erupt

northern women donned the helkappe
the magic hat, the mask, the hood
and, rendered invisible, like ghosts
they moved freely
between life and death
between earth and hell

Hera

Hera
Lady
He-Era the Earth
Rhea
Great Mother
Hiera
Holy One
Erua
who controls birth
The Lady Eire
Eriu
guardian of the applegarden
mother of gods
virgin of spring
mother of summer
crone of autumn
Child
Bride
Widow

How brave and terrible you must be
that they take your name
appropriate it
alter it
call their most fearsome
heroes

Herø
Hera

Io

Io
turning from white to red to black
from virgin to mother to crone
Creator, protector, reaper
Io
Moon
horned goddess
giver of milk
you sail the night skies
watched
by the uncounted millions
of eyes
watched
by stars

Kali

Shiva, who is male
claimed he created human beings
and was the sole parent
the true parent
and
Kali laughed heartily
The spirit of the phallus
challenged
the spirit of the yoni
and each agreed
to create a race of people
without the aid of the other
Shiva
god of the phallus
created the Lingajas who were
"dull of intellect, their bodies feeble
their limbs distorted"
Kali
goddess of the yoni
created the Yonijas
"well-shaped, with sweet aspects
and fine complexions"
Mother Kali
we, your Yonijas
honour you

Kelle

Kelle
most beautiful of women
your robe of cobwebs
shimmering
a spiral pattern of colour
red white black
counterclockwise from toe to head
from earth to heaven
through you and contemplation of you
perfection through meditation
Your sacred fire at Kildare
guarded by women
and St. Kildas Isle
the gateway to your paradise
where the dead rejoice
Kelle
creator protector reaper
mother of the culdees

The warrior priests
the christian invaders insisted
were Irish monks
worshipping the holy child
warrior priests
who resisted the invaders
took to corricles
and went beyond the rim of the world
rather than submit
Kelle
most beautiful of women
westward they sailed
westward
to your paradise

Kleite

Kleite
Amazon queen, founding mother
of the Kleitae, the warrior women
who founded the first city in Italy
Kleite, supposedly reincarnated as a sunflower
turning her face to follow the heat across the sky

Kleite, sometimes pronounced Klute
your name means goddess-like
your name means famous
your name means divine
your name means
clitoris

The city named after you
the city of Clitor
is said to have been sacred
to Artemis
to Demeter
is said to have stood
at the headwaters of Alph
the sacred river
which represented
the menstrual blood of the Mother

Lilith

Lilith
Belit-ili
Belili
Baalat
Divine Lady
Lillake

It is said
Adam married Lilith
because he grew tired
of coupling with beasts

what a man!
what a country!
where men are men
and the sheep are nervous

Adam tried to force Lilith
into the missionary position
the male dominant position
the one-up position
man as heaven
woman on her back

Lilith cursed him
said a magic word
lifted from the earth
flew
to the Gulf of Aqaba

Adam's god sent angels
to bring Lilith to heel
She told them
what she had told Adam
and she continued to consort
with mermaids, magical beasts
giving birth to one hundred children every day

Great mother of agricultural women
resisting the invasions of patriarchal herdsmen
leaving home, fields, crops
rather than forsake the Mother

Lilith
waiting at the gate of the underworld
watching future and past
welcoming the dead

Lilith
Mother of the Lilum
copulating in the dark
with sleeping men
causing
nocturnal emission
loss of power
loss of control
loss of dignity

Lilum
daughters of
Lilith
squatting on men
superior position
their god calls it abomination

Lilim
daughters of Lilith
succubae

Every time a priest
or monk or prelate
or pillar of the community
has a wet dream
Lilith laughs

Lilim
daughters of Lilith
night-hag

Hag
heq
who knows the words of power
the word
Lilith
said to Adam
before she flew

Hag
beautiful
any man visited by you
yearns ever after
searches
burning to own and control
unable to believe
he can never control

Old Woman

Old Woman
Grandmother
Great Grandmother
Midwife
She who draws from the waters
    who brought gods from the seas
who created humanity
Divine midwife
we float in your basket
and in our dreams
know your touch
Akka
MaderAkka
Acca Larentia
so many names
so many titles
for
Great Grandmother
of us all

Old Woman
Crone
Kali the Destroyer
Ceridwen
Atropos the Cutter
Macha
Hecate
Hel
Eresh Kigal
Morgan

Third phase of woman's life
post menopausal
when women no longer flow
the wisdom of the moon
elixir of immortality

but retain it
they attain the gifts of divination
can find water under the earth
grow wonderful gardens
heal ailing animals

Crone
Goddess of Wisdom
Minerva
Athene
Metis
Sophia
Medusa
Old Woman

It is you
soothes our fears
sweeps clean our minds
Men fear you
the slave-women despise you
we
celebrate you

Old woman
crone
bag lady
hag
witch
laughing, toothless
cackling
wait for us!
We are coming
all of us
coming closer to you
daily

Osa

Osa, warrior goddess
you whirl your whip
and the winds respond

Osa, middle daughter
your rainbow robe
splashes against the blue sky
and brings us promise
of retribution
of vengeance
of protection

Twice-born goddess
daughter of wisdom
you rule the storms
the volcanoes
and take the souls of the dead
delivering them back to the sun

Osa
your daughters are secretive
and fiercely protective
of the knowledge

Osa
Macha woman
mixture of water wind and fire
guardian of justice

A thirteen-year-old babysitter
was given a ride home
by the boyfriend of the mother
of the child she had been watching
He beat her for hours
raped her repeatedly
held her captive, tied with a rope
forced on her
anal and oral sex

convicted
he was given three years in jail

Osa
we call on you
inspire us
that we move against that man
and the judge
who sentenced him
so gently

Pomegranate

Rimmon, "pomegranate"
from "rim"
"to give birth"
Rimmon
genital shrine of the Goddess
Pomegranate
red juice/menstrual blood
many seeds/fertility
vulvic shape
Split open
your design
is vaginal
Pomegranate
eaten by the dead
to bring rebirth

First Kings chapter seven verses eighteen to twenty

> And he made the pillars and two rows round about
> upon the one network, to cover the chapiters that
> were upon the top, with pomegranates, and so did
> he for the other chapiter. And the chapiters that
> were upon the top of the pillars were of lily work in
> the porch, four cubits. And the chapiters upon the
> two pillars had pomegranates also above, over,
> against the belly which was by the network; and the
> pomegranates were two hundred in rows round
> about upon the other chapiter

The pillars of Solomon's temple
decorated with female genital symbols
lilies, pomegranates
and Solomon
when alone with the Shulamite woman
drank the juice
of
her pomegranate

Song of Solomon chapter eight verses two and three

I would lead thee
and bring thee into my mother's house
who would instruct me: I would cause thee
to drink the spiced wine
of the juice of my pomegranate
His left hand should be
under my head
and his right hand
should embrace me

Solomon, patriarch
Shulamite woman instructed
by the Mother
Solomon
you are not obeying Adam
Solomon
that is not the missionary position
Shulamite Woman Hail!

Witch

Seer or diviner
from AngloSaxon "witan"
from "vita"
to know
from "vizkr"
clever or knowing one
from
"guiscart"
sagacious one

Early medieval England still had female clan leaders
they kept their matriarchal rights in lawgiving
and law enforcement; the Magna Charta called them
judges
iudices de wich
judges who are witches

In France
many members of the aristocracy and clergy
were involved in and accused of being a witch cult

Unnumbered servants were tortured and burned
for assisting their masters in witchcraft

but in four years not one noble
was tortured or executed

Obviously
it is only poor women who are witches

which is weird
because witches, as we all know,
can turn barnyard manure into pure gold

Little boys get praised for adventurousness
little girls are encouraged
to be quiet, obedient, submissive
and it is considered

very poor taste
to draw attention to one's self
or
one's accomplishments

Perhaps because
a woman of Newbury
knew how to take a wide board
place it on the surface of the river
and surf

Soldiers of the Earl of Essex saw her
and reported
"to and fro she fleeted on the board
standing firm bold upright . . . turning and winding it
which way she pleased, making it passtime to her"

They were so impressed with her agility and daring
they ambushed her, beat her, slashed her head and face
shot her, and left her
"detested carcass to the worms"

(*Women's Encyclopaedia of Myths and Secrets*, p 1078)

Found

At a witch trial in 1593, the investigating gaoler (a married man) apparently discovered the clitoris for the first time, and identified it as a "deavil's teat," sure proof of the witch's guilt. It was "a little lump of flesh, in a manner sticking out as if it had been a teat, to the length of half an inche," which the gaoler "perceiving at the first sight thereof meant not to disclose because it was adjoining to so secret a place which was not decent to be seen; yet in the end, not willing to conceal so strange a matter," he showed it to various bystanders. The bystanders had never seen anything like it either. The witch was convicted.

It is estimated more than 12 million women were burned as witches as Christianity moved across Europe and Britain.

There is no record of how many were convicted because of a clitoris.

(*Women's Encyclopaedia of Myths and Secrets*, p 171)

What Are These Coloured Cones

What are these coloured cones
decorating the temple?
What are these rows
of clay cones coloured
red, white, or black?
What
but the dugs of bitches
swollen with milk
The red-eyed black bitches
of Ceridwen
of Annwn
who pace the periphery
of the underworld
or race the night skies
seeking vengeance
What
but the breasts of maidens
or of mothers
the kelles
who guard, protect, nurture and
eventually
reclaim us
carrying us from this world
to that other
where the scent of appleblossoms
rides the air
and the songs

ah, the songs

so entrance our minds
we lose all earthly conception
of time
and wait the centuries
eating apples
and singing

Annie Poems

Sometimes I Read Magazines

Sometimes
I read magazines, articles, books
written by women
who claim
to be feminist

A woman
could choke on those polysyllabics
could puke on those euphemisms
those polite evasions
and bafflegab convolutions

so much academic jargon
so much blether and real dreck
all of it
politically correct
self proclaimed
spiritually appropriate

Can we not see
how elitist this is
how divisive
how self destructive
suicidal
and
classist
this is?

I admit
I get angry
when upper middle class
white women
presume to present
what they claim
are the opinions of
"our minority sisters"

I want to hear directly from the black women
                 directly from the native women
                 directly from the sisters
who are not a minority
because they are not
minor

When We Meet

when we meet
in bus depots
train stations
at cab stands
airports
coffee shops
theatres
festivals
police stations
television studios
dyke bars
newspaper stands
welfare offices
job interviews
unemployment lines
in hospitals
or union halls
at poetry readings
or riots

the eyes flick
to the throat
the labyris

and the grins
flash
recognition

A Bear Story

I was looking for the honeytree
following the scent on the night air
knowing the stingers would be sleepy
in the cool blackness

There was a woman
naked in the moonlight
her skin gleamed pale
her eyes glittered like stars
she lay on the moss and grass
one hand on her belly
the other beneath her head
and when she saw me
she was unafraid

I wanted to walk lightly
I wanted to dance gracefully
I wished
so much
and she waited
She was unafraid so I was too
and I lumbered close, sniffed carefully
her neck, her underarm, her belly
More fragrant than blossoms, tarter than berries
filling my nostrils, making my head swim
and my belly grow tight and hot
She parted her thighs and smiled
and I found honey without stingers
She gripped my ruff with her fingers
and arched against me, crooning
crooning deep in her throat, eyes closed
breath ragged, and we were there
until the sun was high in the sky

Kyuquot Forest Protectorate

There are trees here stand barkless
their weathered gray exposed wood
twisted and turned upon itself
like a corkscrew, and you know
only the roots sunk deep in the
rocky earth kept these trees from
spiralling away, spinning forever
toward nothing, like those timidly
smiling men with empty faces
who never learned to settle for
any one thing, any one person

Here you learn to be content
with nothing, here you can learn
to exist with sorrow, you can come
face to face with what you have lost
and know keeping something is impossible

The Indians here have eyes like mourners
and their smiles only play at the
edges of their lives, until you feel
they are waiting, and you wonder
                    For What

And sometimes the wind screams at you
days and days of lunatic whining
coming from the mountains and pleading
teasing at your skull, piercing your ears,
winding in and out between your teeth,
until you feel yourself twisting, twisting
like a corkscrew, spinning, spinning
and your roots not yet sunk deep
into the chilling rock soil

Weather Forecast

The Pacific Front
which ought
to have brought
warm weather
          and sunshine
to the island
failed to materialize

The rain and wind
slap at the new cedar siding
and splash against
the large new windows

An old house
renovated
and defying autumn

Inside it
I sit in artificial light
waiting
for warmth

Eleanor's Place

They said we could make a lot of money
Eight acres of strong second growth
fir, cedar, and hemlock
In and out in a couple of weeks, they said
Push the slash in piles and burn it for you, they
      promised
Make good wages just from that big cedar—
don't see many like that any more

I suppose there's a mathematical formula
for figuring out how tall she is
I suppose the length of the shadow
measured at noon, times the square root of
the circumference of the trunk
at ground level, or. . . .
We call her Grandmother. She is so tall
I can imagine her tip
tickling God's toes
She is shaggy and limby, she sways
only in strong winds
She sighs and whispers at night
and the eagle often rests in her boughs
Don't see many like that any more

Small wonder

February

February, and we live under lowhanging gray clouds
in mud to our knees, the woodstove stinking of creosote
our spirits, to steal a phrase from my beloved,
lower than whale shit
In the supermarket lettuce is one dollar eighty a head
lemons sixty-eight cents each, avocados two dollars
      each
and coffee is climbing out of sight
We move between the aisles, caught somewhere
      between anger
and defeat, between outrage and resignation
A woman stands looking into her empty shopping cart
staring at nothing, standing next to the pyramids of
      oranges
and grapefruit, the attractively displayed pineapple,
the mangoes, papayas and chinese pears
Her lips move, her voice is soundless
she stares, talking to herself, she stares
into her empty shopping cart
surrounded by imported fruit
she stares through her shopping cart
into something else
Her kids are in school, her old man
sits in the pub, sipping his slowly warming beer
talking to the guys who used to work in the mill with
      him
talking to the guys who go to the pub for their one beer
      a day
because there's no use going to Manpower
there's no work to be had anywhere, not for the likes of
      them
She stands staring into her shopping cart at nothing
her lips moving, saying nothing
When unemployment insurance is gone
there is welfare, and that's nothing
His job has become nothing
her kids look forward to nothing
her life has become nothing
and lettuce is one dollar eighty a wilted head

Milly

Milly was pregnant at fourteen
Third-generation welfare recipient
she attended grade seven
sometimes
knew nothing of biology
and less of contraception
No marketable job skills
no perceivable options
Her physician agreed to an abortion
The hospital board considered
for ten minutes
Three Roman Catholic businessmen
a Pentecostal school teacher
and a housewife, safely married
to a middleclass white insurance agent
They decided not to approve the application
Milly's physician gave her mood elevators
Her friends gave her everything else
uppers, downers, speeders and
all the smoke she could inhale and blow
The father of the pregnancy
a forty-six year old salmon fisherman
with a wife and three kids, one of them
two years older than Milly
had no intention of divorce and remarriage
no intention of losing his house
stationwagon, four-by, trailer, and outboard
Told Milly to take a walk. A long one
Her depression deepened, she turned to her mother
who poured her a drink, lit a cigarette,
and said, Welcome to the world, kid
They sat together often
the rye bottle between them
while Milly's mother
talked of deja vu
and yelled at the other kids
to put a lid on the noise goddammit
Milly ate Kraft Dinner and Hamburger Helper
two-day-old reduced price bread
canned weiners and beans

and watched a lot of television
She particularly liked Waltons re-runs
Little House on the Prairie and game shows
where people suddenly won new cars
trips to exotic places and a year's supply of Miss Mew
When she felt hungry for something
she could not identify
she unwrapped a Mars Bar
and dreamed of Olympic gold
of admiring crowds of acceptance and
something else she couldn't identify
The night her son was born
Milly screamed for hours; shit shit shit
She took him back to her mother's rented house
and left him in the care of her sister
Then went down to welfare
to apply for the fourth generation
still muttering shit shit shit shit shit shit shit shit shit
     shit shit shit shit shit

Without Prejudice

It isn't easy to try to convince yourself you're sane
when what everybody knows
is what nobody will investigate
Everybody knows there's an elementary school
      principal
who got himself into one of his students
and got her pregnant. She was fourteen, everybody
      knows that
Or at least everybody says everybody knows
Fourteen, and still in elementary school
so you can figure out how bright she was, how mature,
      how stable
Fourteen, still in elementary school
and hustled by the principal. She got pregnant. Her
      family
was old-world, everybody knows that, and so ashamed
they left town
Everybody knows he's still here, still principal
Everybody knows nothing was done
Everybody talks about it over coffee and gingerbread,
over tea and banana loaf, over beer in the pub, at craft
      fairs
and blackberry festivals, at bus stops and in coffee
      shops
Sooner or later, usually sooner, someone talks about
      what
everybody knows

But if you write a letter to a school district official
asking why it is everybody knows this
but nothing has been done
you'll get a letter back
explaining the laws of libel and slander

Everybody knows that what everybody knows
is what nobody will investigate. Which makes
      everybody
feel baffled, frustrated, and very fatalistic

My darling knows. Tells me it might even be a good
        thing
After all, he's sure teaching the kids reality

Sea Fair, Powell River

You don't get many chances to see heroism first hand
It's not as if there were knights chasing dragons or
crusaders fighting infidels or brave stands to be taken
in defence of freedom, god, flag, motherhood, and
        blackberry pie
All the mountains around here have been climbed,
        clear-cut logged,
eroded, wasted, raped, and desecrated. There are no
        Everests
or Kilimanjaros here, no Alps to ski or anything like
        that
We live under a pall of mill scunge, the rain more acid
        every year
and the biggest stand we've taken in years
is to declare this a nuclear weapons free zone. And hope
the idea spreads to include Washington and Leningrad
You don't get many chances to see heroism first hand

So there we were, in line for food, and all around us
are kids with balloons, hot dogs, corn on the cob
kids with smiles, kids with greasy faces, kids laughing
and over there the loggers sports are unwinding
chain saws howling, sawdust flying
some guy is racing up a peeled pole, spurs digging
arm straining to ring the bell,
over here chokermen are racing to set the beads
out on the water the dozerboats are warming up
and in front of us
two women, two kids, and a man, waiting for food
Two normal ordinary everyday-looking women
Two boys in training to be patriarchs
And the smiling self-contented role model of
uppermiddleclass pillar of the community
socially acceptable respectability
and suddenly
my love, at the top of her voice, is going on about
something, body rigid, and I don't have a clue
not even the beginning of a clue
what it is she's saying

—Makes you wonder—she shouts—why anybody
would DO a thing like that! I mean, name of heaven, a
grown man? Messing around with a KID? A person
couldn't do a disgusting thing like that and be
NORMAL, would you think?—

  the two women in front of us stiffen
  the older one turns and glares fiercely
  the kids walk off quickly
  the balding blond in the rainbow teeshirt gets
    redder
  and redder and redder until you'd think his ears
    would explode

—I understand—my beloved hollers—that the guys
who fuck children have penises so small only a kid
would be impressed. No intelligent adult woman—she
roars—would do anything but bust out laughing—

Someone in the lineup behind us clears her throat
    hesitantly
Clears her throat again, then, in a voice nearly choked
    silent by conditioning
manages, "I heard that, too. About their dicks being so
    small, I mean"
A man in the lineup laughs, his laugh is smothered by
    an older woman
who begins to explain, loudly, how it was, back on the
    farm
in Saskatchewan, you took a tom cat and shoved him
    headfirst
into an old gumboot, until only his tail and his testicles
    showed
"Doesn't take much," she bellows to nobody in
    particular
"You can use an old razor blade if that's all you've got"

—The one thing I REALLY cannot understand—my
darling screeches—is how any woman could possibly
continue to live with any man when she knew he

diddled little girls. You'd think—she finishes—you'd
think she'd have more self respect than to live with a
pervert—

You don't get many chances to see heroism first hand
but when you do, you recognize it
You know it for what it really is when five foot three
stands up to six foot two and names what everyone
        knows
and nobody discusses

Sometimes I look at her
and all I can think is
"more guts than a slaughterhouse"

but I don't suppose
she'll ever get a medal

Did you know the word "hero"
was stolen from us? It used to be
"hera," just like the goddess Hera
"the holy one" "the Earth"
"the mother of the gods" the ruler
of the apple-orchard of immortality

And so, instead of giving her a medal
I planted apple trees. I prune them
I fuss over them, I fertilize them
and every spring there will be blossoms

I mean you don't see Heraism first hand very often
so when you do, you should give it some importance
validate it

Even small Heraisms
are a big deal. Or ought to be

In Class I Am Asked

In class I am asked if I know of a group of women
who meet to give each other support and to share
        experiences
help each other with the problems attendant upon
separation and divorce
If there is one, I don't know about it. There was a
rape assault line, there were volunteers willing to try
to help women put together their shattered lives
but the line dissolved
in a sea of absolute community apathy
—you'd think nobody here had anything to fear—
—you'd think guys like Leo didn't even live here—
—you'd think good old Bob was a decent human being—
—you'd think the goddam women would have better sense!—
There's a safe house, now, but how safe is it
when the town is so small
the batterers
know where the safe house is
and know
the women who try to run it? How safe is it
when a lawyer says there's no way a judge
can convict, and a social worker agrees with him
in spite of all evidence to the contrary?
Who is a terrified woman going to believe?
Some unofficial woman who says yes
or official men who say no?
They say a society gets the government and services
it deserves
The police here grew up on Coke and Twinkies
in towns exactly like this one
from sea to sea ad mare usque ad mari
You expect women to believe
those police will protect them?

Whenever A Woman Forgets Herself

Whenever a woman forgets herself
and raises her voice
whenever a woman protests an insult
or resists a rapist
or insists on vengeance
or says No, dammit, I won't!

my mother laughs

Whenever a religious sister
puts aside her veil and habit
and goes over the wall
because
she began to ask questions
and in the asking realized

my mother laughs

Whenever a woman
refuses to be informer
or ignorant
or invisible

my mother
laughs

When Next in Soft Dark or Bright Light

When next
in soft dark or bright light
you taste
with trembling tongue
that gift
and sanctity

think of the ocean
lapping rhythmic
each wave
responding
to the pull of the moon
of the salt scented fog
of iodine rich spray
spattering
against your cheeks
of kelp glistening brown
tossed on pink granite rocks

taste fully
inhale deeply

Have you ever seen the western horizon
pink and silver, pale blue and lavender
and purple night
rising
from the tossing sea?

Have you ever
tasted your lover
until both of you
began to shimmer
silver
and a high thin noise
not heard but felt filled the room
wrapping you both
in vibrating
energy

while rich purple night
rises from the waves
absorbing
the colours of sunset
wrapping the world
in her

purple?

When next you are with your lover
lie quiet, feeling the smooth
warmth of her thighs
against your cheeks
the brushy thatch
against your forehead

Open your eyes
and think
of an apple sliced in half
the core pattern
seeded rich
of pomegranates
glistening, juice filled
of fresh figs
iris flowers
lilies
and milkweed pods

Think
of eighty thousand Celts
who died protecting
    this magic
of twelve million witches
burned
for worshipping thus

Remember
we were not always cursed
we will not accept
invisibility

Remember
who and what we were
              and will be again

and love
worthily

I Am She Who in Other Times

I am she who in other times
wore her hair unbound, her body unfettered
I am she who proudly displayed
her menstrual blood and taught her sons
that a woman in her cycle was sacred
I am she who moved where she wished
and worked at her craft
choosing lovers for her own reasons
keeping her children for herself
forming her own family
making her own choices

I am she who built her shelter
and at the doorway placed
the circle of stones
I am she who dug her firepit
and protected it
carried her infant slung on her back
and gave suck openly
I am she who honoured the mothers
and the aunties and the grandmothers
who honoured the Mother
above all

I am she who danced following the moon
and sang at night, who drank barley beer
and ate barley bread, who set snares,
baited traps, tanned hides, and
ate the meat she caught for herself
I am she who wore the crescent moon
and was bathed in woad. I am she
who guarded the thirteen pillars
and waited
for the round corricles which bore
the bodies of the Sisters

I am she who left regret
to the cowardly, who lifted the dead
and was not afraid. I am she who
bathed them and prepared them

then escorted them
to the hidden mounds. I am she
who opened the mouth of the underground
and walked inside
singing
I am she who placed the departed
with their sisters and left food for them
recounted the events since the last visit
left gifts and even
sang them songs, told them jokes
that they would remember us
with fondness

I am she who in other times
watched the watch fires
and dreamed my dreams
I am she who trusted her visions
and who laughed
at the invaders
I am so unafraid of death
I did not hesitate
to explore life
I am she so familiar with death
I acknowledged it a part
of my purpose
I am she
the invader feared

I am she, so familiar with death
I have died many times
and been born
again
and
again
and
again

each time re-learning
what I have always known

that they fear me
that they hate me
that they
wish even now
to destroy me

I am she who in other times
knew
and who today
knows

I am the knife
I am the mound
I am the orb
I am the wand

I
dyke

I mother
dyke

When I Was Very Small

When I was very small my uncle said
You'll never get into heaven
if your shoes aren't shined
Never get into heaven?
Have to go to hell?
I buffed and polished
religiously
Now
I fear neither heaven nor hell
and I still buff and polish
My sweetie laughs
particularly on those days
when I take it into my head
to oxblood polish
my work boots
Well, I rationalize, it's
very good for the leather
it makes it last much longer
and when your life has been
povertystricken
you learn to make things last
as long as possible
Besides, I mutter, some animal
died
to provide this leather
(I have found self-rightousness
is often a wonderful defence tactic)

What it really is, you know,
is the years of hearing
those disgusting
barefoot and pregnant jokes

I am not pregnant
never will be again
and a dyke with shiny shoes
sure as hell
is not barefoot!

Life Does Not Consist of a Series of Orgasms

Life does not consist of a series of orgasms
complete with the Mormon Tabernacle choir singing
      Alleluia
while volcanoes erupt and mountains quiver, the earth
      splits
and the trapeze star does a triple-gainer, a double
      somersault
and a back flip, then lands safely on delicate feet

There was a time I thought words meant what words
      were supposed to mean
and that words were a way to communicate
Now I agree with the friend who said people who love
      words the most
trust them the least

"Relationship." We've heard that word so many times
we all think we know what it means. People have
good relationships, long-standing relationships,
bad relationships, destructive relationships,
with family, friends, lovers

The word has become like a threadbare pair of jeans
no warmth, no utility, no comfort
our backsides poking from the wornout seat
a tatterass embarrassment

I'm not having a relationship with you
I don't want to repeat any relationship stuff I've
      experienced

If one more clown does one more triple gainer, double
      somersault
and a back flip, I may spit up on my sneakers

Look at what Relationships have been, have meant
and I won't even bother with the seventeen year
      marriage
half of all the books published in the past ten years
have examined that litany of disillusion

Let's look instead at those supposed volcanoes:
one woman wanted me to promise I would publish
no explicit love poetry that might make anyone
think I was writing of, for, because of, or to
her
The sex was terrific, and there is something so
invigorating
about not knowing where you stand at any given time
not knowing if it's going to be gentle words
or demanding sentences, winning smiles, or floods
of scalding tears, but it all came to a tacky stop
when I said no, and her gorgeous hands
grabbed my throat, leaving marks I covered with
a turtleneck for two weeks—I can take a hint—
Or what about the one who made love incredibly
then afterward brooded and examined her guilt?
Or the one who made a habit of drinking enough
Scotch to put her on her knees horking into the bowl?
She at least understood why I lost interest
She had a drinking problem, but it hadn't destroyed her
        brain
Is it a relationship when someone lies to you?
Shows up after a two-week holiday with a big smile
and a warm hug, then, smiling and laughing, tells
you she went skinnydipping with friends, and
someone had a two month old baby, and it started
to cry, she picked it up to comfort it and it
nuzzled at her sunwarmed skin
and left a huge hickey so purple it was almost black
on the curve of her breast
I don't expect you'd swallow that one either
I think it amazed and even insulted her
when I shrugged
and said
Kids do the damnedest things
Is it a relationship when someone tries charming
        manipulation
and when it doesn't get her what she wants
she lies on the floor and howls
or sits
wailing and banging her head on the radiator?
What about someone who says on Tuesday afternoon

she wants to find a house so you can move in together
invites you to supper, explains she has a meeting she
has to attend but invites you to watch TV and wait
until she gets back, and, when leaving, kisses your
        cheek
and says, smiling, you don't have to sit up, you know,
you could warm up the bed. So you do the dishes, clean
up the kitchen, eventually go to bed. Fall asleep, in
fact, only to be awakened at three-thirty as she sneaks
into the house and tiptoes to the other bedroom
where she undresses in the dark and gets into bed alone
Then is mad as a wet hen when you just get up, get
        dressed
and leave her house, go back to your own, unplug the
        phone
and go to bed properly. Told me I had no right to judge
Told me I didn't know the details. Told me I had no
        right
to tell her I didn't want to know the details. Accused me
of isolating her because I wouldn't even try to
        understand
the intensity of her relationship with him
I'm sure his wife wouldn't understand it either
Pitched a fit and jumped into the middle of it
when I said I refused to be involved with any woman
so unable to make a decision she didn't know if she
wanted to sleep with a dyke or a man. Called me
        "obtuse"
Whatever in hell she meant by that!
When I think about it I begin to wonder
why so much of my life has been tangled with crazies
Am I a magnet attracting them?
Or are they magnets attracting me?
But they all said we were having a Relationship

Thank god we are not having a Relationship
I don't want to have a Relationship with you
We've been together almost five years
and I much prefer having a Life

Relationships can make you crazy
but Life
is what keeps me sane

For Eleanor: First Poem in More Than a Year

When I was little, no more than six or seven
a neighbour came to visit, to have lunch and
chat with my mother. Salmon salad and five bean salad
and tea in the thin cups that almost never left the shelf
poured from a pot so thin you could see the darkness
        inside
the line of tea lowering cup by cup

My mother scrubbed my hands and face
stuffed me into a pale dress with a flower design
and I wore all my best manners and a ribbon in my hair

Privy, for the first time, to the talk and laughter of
        women
I kept all my best manners firmly in place
although the ribbon slipped from my hair
and my feet dangled inches above the floor

Only after she had gone and the cups and saucers
once again safe in their special place on the shelf
did I ask
why is she so fat?

A pause   Then my mother said, She's going to have a
        baby
A pause   And I asked, So? Why is she so fat?

My mother told me the big fat lump was where the baby
lived, curled, she said, right under the mommy's heart
Put there, she said, by love

I remember standing on a chair in front of the
square porcelain sink that never quite came clean
an old apron over my slightly soiled good dress
holding the spoons and forks and dull knives
staring into the eye of   magic

Not daring to ask what I suddenly
so desperately needed to know

She hugged me, her hands still soapy and wet
her head lowered so our cheeks touched
She smelled of so many good things
of warmth and sunlight and devilled egg
and of something else, for which I had no name

Yes, she answered the unasked. You were like
a willow leaf before it opens, curled
up like a kitten, and when you finally came
from under my heart, you brought all that love with
    you

I, of course, thought that the love that had put me there
was her love for me

Last night you cuddled me and talked softly
your lips against my breast
and when you laughed, your breath was warm
and damp against my skin

I fell asleep in the soft sureness of your love
your small brown hand curled like a leaf
beneath my heart

Osa

So there we were living in houses
side by each at the corner of
Terminal Avenue and Dawes Street
you with your three black kids
me with my three pinkie kids
and not a man
of any colour,
shape, size, or inclination
anywhere to be seen

You told me your name
was an old family name
but you didn't know
anything more about it

Well, years have passed
and all those kids
have grown up and gone
off on their own

and guess what

She was a goddess!

Margaret

I guess you suppose
I don't know what
they think about me
in town

I guess you think
I don't know
what they say
about me
in town

I know I'm fat
and drink too much
I know the loggers
only buy me beer
so they can
get into me

I know they wear rubbers
so they won't catch
a disease

I got no disease
but I don't tell 'em

When they wear rubbers
I don't have to feel
their skin
in me

I know what they think

Well
    so what

I've seen vampires
suckin' at my throat
and leeches on my skin
I've heard Buckwus yell
in the night
and listened to four kids

dyin' in a fire
I had a husband once
but that was a mistake
My whole life's been one fuckin' mistake
after another

But never the same one twice

I guess you think I don't know

I know

and I don't give a shit

ii
She just walked in the
house is all
her eyes eating holes
in her face
the way all madwomen's eyes do
"I gotta have some water," she said
"Gimme a loan of a bucket"
and we did
She came back
no more than five minutes later
even crazier than before
"I can't put it out," she said
"Maybe you could help me
Everyone else is asleep, you see"

They'd all been asleep
or drunk
or both
and the oil lamp
tipped
The baby yelling
woke her up
but
she couldn't get
into the room

So she went mad
and came to our place
looking for a bucket

Every Now and Again Something Happens

Every now and again something happens
that drives home what I have always known
and the truth is again
underlined for emphasis

You came to have tea and visit
and then asked me
forthright as always
if there was any chance I was going to
change my mind

And I said no
I owed you the truth
I have always owed you
at least the truth

I expected
sorrow or
anger or
anything except
the way your eyes flooded with tears
and you smiled
the way you smiled forty years ago
when life was insane
and I was confused
and you
were
sanctuary

And you said, Oh, I am so glad!

The tears slipped down your face
and I knew
it was the first time
I had ever seen you cry

You said
I was so afraid for so long
that you were going to just

give in
and be
whoever it was
they thought you ought to be
instead of
who you were intended to become

I have made it a point recently
to say now how much I love you
Too often we wait
until it is too late
to say it to
the one who really matters

How Old Was I That Year?

How old was I that year? Six? Seven?
That year I lived with my northenglish grandmother
and her mad alcoholic son
and saw my mom only occasionally
Was it really as carnival bizarre and frightening as I
    now recall?
I have this absolutely clear recollection of being
on the main street in Ladysmith
and coming down the hill toward us
half a dozen roman catholic nuns
their long black habits whipping in the wind
I'd never seen anything like that before, and gaped
My grandmother grabbed me, turned me around, held
    me
so my face was pressed against her belly
Her body, always so soft and cuddly
suddenly rigid, like a barn cat with kittens
who has just spotted a stray dog
When the nuns had gone by my grandma told me
if ever I saw them and I was alone I was to run
Run, she said, as fast as tha feet will tek thee
And that woman who was my comfort, that dear
    woman
who reinforced every idea I have about love and
kindness, that woman who believed God not only
existed but cared, told me the nuns just waited
for the chance to find a child alone, especially
a little girl. And then, she said, they'll scoop
you. Hide you under their big skirts and be off with you
and nobody, she warned, nobody will ever know

That was the year questions never quite got answered
That was the year questions just gave birth to more
    questions
What it is, he said, is there's a very very few
who sit up top with all the money, and they
are the Fitznoodle Buggeries
Just under them are a few more, they claim they're
related to the Fitznoodle Buggeries but they're not
not in the least little bit. They're the Von Hoffenpuffins

Beneath the Von Hoffenpuffins are quite a few
who claim to be related. And who knows,
maybe they are. But not to the Fitznoodle Buggeries!
And under them, the Von Hoitentoiten-Huffen-
    Pufferies
are the MucketyMucks. Who aren't related to, but work
    for,
all the others every chance they get. Below the
    MucketyMucks
are the BigWig Highpockets. Actually, they're nobody
    at all but
they certainly think they are. Then there's some other
basically no accounts, like the Hoi Polloi and the
    Boor-zhwah-zee
and down near the bottom, there's us
And the funny thing
He paused and looked around to be sure nobody was
    eavesdropping
cautiously sharing the secret of all times
privileging me with wisdom from generation to
    generation
The funny thing is
us at the bottom
are directly related
to the Fitznoodle Buggeries!

He laughed, then. From the gut, roiling with cheap
    whiskey
up through a throat made raw by home-rollie cigarettes
past snuff stained teeth
hot jagged laughter, and the smell of sweat
smell of booze
smell of tobacco
smell of
something

something that only a few years later
stopped his laughter forever
replaced it with something else
something so like self loathing it was contagious
and most of the rest of us caught it too

Here, you, she said, laughing and twisting my hair into
    pigtails
just you hold still. We can't all go racing around the
    countryside
with our hair blowing wild as if we'd never heard of
    christianity!
It's your crowning glory, she said, and it's only proper it
    be tidy
What would the world come to, anow, if we all ran
    around
like raggletaggle gypsies? There, she said, that's much
    better
You look like my own dear darling girl now that you're
    tidy

I do declare, she snapped, you've more questions, miss
than the Witch of Endor has answers!
Give over wi'it! Eh, tha'd talk the ears off a field of corn!

Here, you, fix thy face. If yon clock strikes when tha's
    got
that look on tha face, that's it, tha'll stay like that
    forever!

Eh, well, what's this, then? Tears?
Ah, lassie there's no need to cry now, save thy tears
for when tha's older. Tha'll need'em all
Come then, sit on my lap. . . if thee can find it!
That's better
Remember, dearie, God's in his heaven, all's right with
    the world

Annie

The trouble with having a poet for a mother
is the unrealistic view of the world she gives you
Annie told me menstruation
was the weeping of the disappointed womb

Years later I said
they were probably tears of relief

and she looked at me as if life
had, again, disappointed her

If I Was Ten My Brother Was Seven and Annie Was Not Yet Thirty

If I was ten my brother was seven and Annie was not yet
    thirty
She'd had her life smash before her eyes more than
    once
had picked up the shards, tried to put them together
and carried on the best she could

Sometimes, today, I hear educated young women
blithely discussing Perceivable Options
and I wonder what Annie would have seen

She was putting fragments back together again,
    working at the hospital
working for minimum wage, walking a half hour to
    work, working a long shift
walking that half hour back home again, to two kids,
    and the one
who danced and sang and charmed and smiled and hit a
    lot
Somehow, alchemy or self-denial, or both
she had saved enough money
to take us to the PNE

our reward, she said, for being so helpful
for doing without, and not whining about it

I only wish, she said
I could do more for you
    give more to you

She bought us new clothes, new underwear,
new socks, and new Sisman Scampers
packed all our stuff in a small suitcase
and walked with us through the early morning softness
to the CP terminal. Only the dogs and cats and us
were awake, and all the lawns were dew-damp
Spider webs glistened like trapped diamonds in
    someone's lilac

We had breakfast on the boat
white tablecloths thicker than winter sheets
real silver forks and knives, the silver cream jug
engraved with C P R
and a waiter with a towel over his arm, smiling at Annie

In Vancouver we walked up a hill
past the statue of a soldier with a gun
Who's he? asked my brother
Nobody knows, she said, but he died for you
Why? he asked. He was a hero, she said
and I think she still believed that back then

We left our suitcase in the room at the Alcazar Hotel
and rode the bus to the PNE
There was so much there
I can't remember a single thing
just colour and noise and people and feeling lucky

I wonder
now that I'm older than Annie was then
I wonder what she'd gone without to give us
that weekend reward for not whining

We ate at the Sky Diner. They've torn it down since
Done like an airplane, they even had scenic pictures
        rolling constantly
behind a frame that looked like a porthole
See, Annie laughed, we're as well off as millionaires
we can have supper and look at the Rockies, with a bit
        of imagination
we can tour the entire country. And we played Pretend
        all through
the meal, ate our dessert in Halifax, Nova Scotia
then stepped through the door
to a Vancouver city sidewalk

Annie always set great store by the imagination
It's your ticket, she said, to anywhere you want to be

We slept three to a bed that night
the sounds of the city riding on the fresh air

through the partly-open window
Stale air brings bad dreams, she said

In the morning we had a bath, dried ourselves
with big thick white towels autographed Alcazar
Annie was dressed and helping stuff my brother into
his new clothes while I sat on the windowsill
watching the traffic and all those people in the streets

Screech of brakes, a form falling
arms like wings of a grouse shot in mid-air
flailing uselessly
A lady got hit by a car, I yelled

And Annie ran

I sat rooted to the windowsill, watching
all those people standing, just standing, useless.
    Useless

Then there was Annie
in her second-best cotton dress
talking to all those useless people
the way she talked to us. Ordering. Calmly

Go to the hotel desk and phone the ambulance
Stand back and give her air
Make sure the driver is all right
You, yes you, make them all stay back, she doesn't need
    anyone
stepping on her face
You'll be fine, dear, it's okay, the ambulance will be
    here any minute now, just breathe, that's it, in and
    out and in and out, that's it, you're fine

The policeman came and everyone moved away
He watched Annie working on the injured woman
Move on, he said, we've got a nurse here
Everything is fine

And when the ambulance came
They said everything Annie had done
was just exactly the right thing

Annie wasn't a nurse
Annie worked in the kitchen

I was so proud. Exactly the right thing, they said

I only wish, she said
I could do more for you
        give more to you